The Scriptures

A Gallery Of Poems by Eric Lamont Norris

To order additional copies of this book, contact:
Xlibris Corporation
1-888-795-4274
www.Xlibris.com
Orders@Xlibris.com

~There is art in everything. It is up to the eye of the beholder to realize that it is there.

~Eric Lamont Norris

I'm Goin' Down

~Now for the past two months,
I was full of **infatuation**,
All I ever needed or wanted was some sensual **persuasion**.
Text after text got even more **intense**,
My feelings grew more and more after each **kiss**.
Whenever I saw you, my soul grew with **excitement**,
Never mind all the others, you're the most **consistent**,
Not just your **persistence**,
But also your **existence**.
Before you left for a break, I gave you two **gardens**,
And after you left, I heard you had to think about **things**.
While you were gathering your thoughts,
I was left to **worry**,
All the stress would kill me,
it would be me they would have to **bury**,
This time was **scary**,
I began to get **weary**,
Anticipating bad news would make me **teary**.
This didn't happen in a week, I didn't have seven **days**,
It was nine days, damn it was hard in many **ways**,
Staring out my window, looking in a **daze**,
Waiting for you to determine our **fate**,
First day of the next week, already back from **break**,
Hearing your voice was what I had to **anticipate**.

Most of the day had past, until that **evening**,
During this time, you uttered words
that were very **shocking**.
You started off saying that I was **perfect**,
But if I were so perfect, why did I have to hear
something like **this**.
You proceeded to say that there was something **missing**,
When all this time, I thought you had
developed some **feelings**.
You said you didn't want me to be hurt in the **future**,
It's too late, I'm hurting because of your early **departure**.
You weren't ready for a relationship,
so you took yourself **out**,
I thought there was a spark,
but all it is right now is stalked **out**.
It can't get any worse than this, I prematurely **thought**,
But there's something else you mentioned,
it happened to be a **song**.
You said it would explain everything that you **felt**,
I had to hear this tune, it couldn't be **withheld**.
The song was alright at first, it started off real **cool**,
But the finale of the chorus put me in low **mood**.
It started off with I being everything that you **wanted**,
It ended with me meaning nothing to you,
and then we **parted**.
People keep telling me things to make me get over **you**,
I hope they understand that it's not that **simple**.
I tried to open up my heart, but you closed the **door**,
How do I feel right now, it doesn't matter **anymore**.

Aftermath

~How many times has something bad happened to me?
Leaving me in this state of being sad and unhappy.
I've got to realize that my life ain't close to being done,
Tomorrow's another day, it'll be a better one.

As I sit here in my room,
Thinking will it end soon,
Pain and stress within me put me in this mood.
Day after day, I try to deal with it,
It be hurting me more than just a little bit.
I be thinking to myself that I'm going through this all alone,
Things not going my way is really starting to get old,
Hang in there son, is what I am being told,
So I keep waiting for some good luck to finally unfold.
My family is what keeps me positive,
They're one of the reasons why I continue to live.
I try to keep things that bother me, trapped inside,
To be unhappy and sad is not how I want to live my life.
The saying goes find happiness in each and every day,
To do this all the time, it's harder than they say.
There are several ways to set myself free,
I just have to pick the right option for me.
Things are bothering me, work be stressing me,
Girls are stressing me, friends be stressing me,
School is stressing me, everything is stressing me,
Lord almighty, God please keep blessing me.
Why is it that I keep holding on to stress?
I can't seem to let it go, like all of the rest.
I guess I'm weak, I keep getting down on myself,
Feeling bad for myself,
This is bad for my health.

If my life ended right now, did I live it to the fullest?
If I were to answer back no, then it would be bullshit.
I've been so many places,
Seen so many faces,
To have lived this long, I'm glad that I made it.
Speaking of death, I wonder if I were dead,
Would they be happy or sad, or is it all in my head?
Now I would much rather, live than die,
But if I died, would they laugh or would they cry?
Talk about me good and true, or bad with lies?
Shed those tears from their eyes, as my soul flies?
I know that my family would truly miss me,
But the rest of them, would they give a damn about me?
One less bedroom, one less mouth to feed,
One less black man, one less human being.
I've got a big heart, I have no room for hate,
For my family, I'll put my life at stake.
I've got so much more than me, myself and I,
Why am I dying to live if I'm just living to die?

How many times has something bad happened to me?
Leaving me in this state of being sad and unhappy.
I've got to realize that my life ain't close to being done,
Tomorrow's another day; it'll be a better one.

Rollin' Solo

~There are so many fine women in this world,
I'm wondering if I can find that perfect girl.
I've been searching so very high, and searching so very low,
But my success is coming awfully slow.
So many women in the past have deceived me,
I'm beginning to wonder if my destiny is to be lonely.
Lord why is it that the fine women are always taken,
Why do the good girls stay with the pricks, will they awaken.
In one instant, you could be out there wanting somebody,
Not a single one in sight, they all have somebody.
The next instant, you finally find someone,
Then all the ones you desired, want you to be the one.
Is it that I have nothing good to offer?
Or do they look at me, and say "why bother"?
Maybe I'm too young to experience a romantic encounter,
Last time I checked, I thought age was just a number.
Is it wrong to despise all of my exes?

Keep in mind that they broke me, left me all a mess.
I've experienced most of the alphabet, including J and V,
Can't forget the N and K, unfortunately.
Some of these girls, I can't bear to see their face,
Because I know their true selves, and it's a disgrace.
But who's to say it's just them, it could be me,
Maybe it's something about me
that made them decide to deceive.
After each ex, I sat and thought what I did wrong,
What could I have done better, so that I could
be singing a different song?
I now look at it one way, and one way only,
It's nobody's fault, it's all about compatibility.
But this is what life's all about, the highs and lows,
That's just the way it is, it can't be controlled,
So despite what has happened in the past,
and me feeling low,
I know it won't be long before I'm done, rollin' solo.

I Want You To Be
My Girlfriend

~I want you to be my girlfriend,
I'm so into you,
The Lord knows how bad I want to be with you,
I know it's sudden but I felt that you should know my truth,
I fell in love with you the moment I laid eyes on you.
And I just felt that my confession could not stay within,
Baby, I want you to be my girlfriend.

Yes, I'll say it again, I want you to be my girl,
As soon as I saw you, you threw my heart for a swirl.
I would've told you sooner, but I didn't want to scare you away,
Whenever I see your pretty face, all my worries just wash away.
Whenever you get close to me, I lock up and my body gets weak,
I see you being a lady in the streets, I wonder if in the bed you're
a freak.
You're always on my mind, go ahead call it an obsession,
But with her and I, I feel we've got a connection.
I connect with you in many ways, emotionally and mentally,
But I keep dreaming of us connecting sexually and sensually.
After I tell you this, I know I won't regret it,
About you and I, just allow me to say…
I want you to be my girlfriend.

Girl everything you do, puts a smile on my face,
Whether you send me a text, or touch me in any way.
Girl, if we were in elementary school, I would write you a note,
It doesn't matter how I ask you, just as long as you know.
I want to be the man in your life, and you the girl in mine,
I don't want a one night stand or fling, I want you for all time.
Every moment we spend together, it tops the last,
It doesn't matter what we do, with you I have a blast.
My mind, body and soul are complete as soon as I hold you,
I'll tell you how I feel in any language, like "Te quiero".
After I tell you this, I know I won't regret it,
About you and I, just allow me to say…
I want you to be my girlfriend.

My girlfriend…you know I want you,
My girlfriend…you know I need you,
My girlfriend…you know I love you.

I want you to be my girlfriend,
I'm so into you,
The Lord knows how bad I want to be with you,
I know it's sudden but I felt that you should know my truth,
I fell in love with you the moment I laid eyes on you.
And I just felt that my confession could not stay within,
Baby, I want you to be my girlfriend.

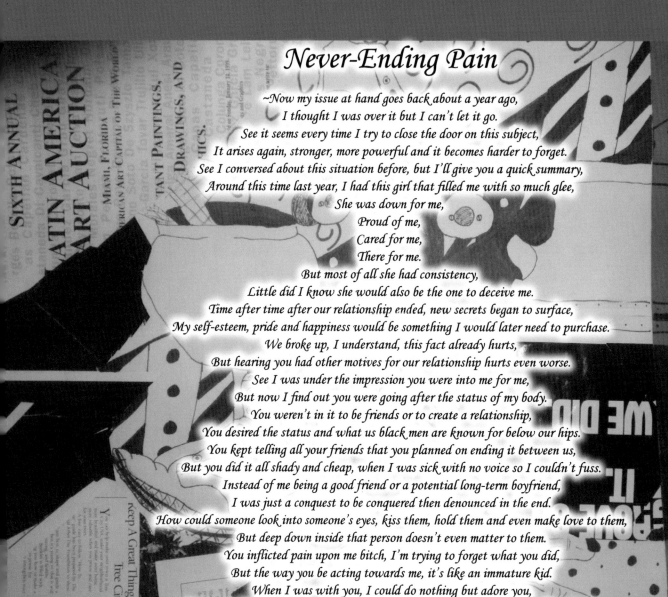

Never-Ending Pain

~Now my issue at hand goes back about a year ago,
I thought I was over it but I can't let it go.
See it seems every time I try to close the door on this subject,
It arises again, stronger, more powerful and it becomes harder to forget.
See I conversed about this situation before, but I'll give you a quick summary,
Around this time last year, I had this girl that filled me with so much glee,
She was down for me,
Proud of me,
Cared for me,
There for me.
But most of all she had consistency,
Little did I know she would also be the one to deceive me.
Time after time after our relationship ended, new secrets began to surface,
My self-esteem, pride and happiness would be something I would later need to purchase.
We broke up, I understand, this fact already hurts,
But hearing you had other motives for our relationship hurts even worse.
See I was under the impression you were into me for me,
But now I find out you were going after the status of my body.
You weren't in it to be friends or to create a relationship,
You desired the status and what us black men are known for below our hips.
You kept telling all your friends that you planned on ending it between us,
But you did it all shady and cheap, when I was sick with no voice so I couldn't fuss.
Instead of me being a good friend or a potential long-term boyfriend,
I was just a conquest to be conquered then denounced in the end.
How could someone look into someone's eyes, kiss them, hold them and even make love to them,
But deep down inside that person doesn't even matter to them.
You inflicted pain upon me bitch, I'm trying to forget what you did,
But the way you be acting towards me, it's like an immature kid.
When I was with you, I could do nothing but adore you,
But your silent treatment, avoiding me and acting immature are boring things to do.
For the longest time I held no grudges or hard feelings,
You just made an enemy out of me, this is just the beginning.

Darlin'

~Darlin',
My darlin'.
Oh how I miss you,
Now I feel like the color of the sky, that's blue.
That song which is your voice,
Is music to my ears,
But when your song becomes mute,
It brings me to tears
Darlin',
My darlin'
That sculpture of yours which is your body,
I love to reach out my arms to hold,
But when you're not here,
I'm left to feel all alone.
Oh how I wish someone would reach out to me,
And restore happiness within me,
Wherever you are, I hope you're smiling down on me,
With you like old times, is where I want to be.
Darlin'
My darlin',
No one knows the pain I'm in,
Because you not being with me is a loss, not a win.
As I sit here on this bench,
A cool breeze blows through the trees,
I'm alone filled with sorrow,
Darlin' I'm missing thee.

Darlin',
My darlin',
You are more than in my mind,
And from now until the end of time.
Wherever we are, we'll never be apart,
See my darlin', you are in my heart.
Darlin',
My darlin'
I can't seem to glare up at the sky,
Because when I see the sunshine, I begin to cry.
Darlin',
My darlin'
Will this pain of mine ever end?
So I can be comfortable from within.
I want you to know that you're in my heart,
And I hope that we never part.
Darlin'
My darlin'
Darlin'
My darlin'

My Addiction

~Yeah baby, you know it's you I like,
You make me smile, and drive me wild,
I want to rock your world,
Damn I love having you as my girl,
You're my addiction.

Baby you're graceful like the night sky,
You catch my eye,
Damn I love it that you are mine,
For all time,
Whenever I'm with you, I feel high,
When you come by,
When we ride,
It's fly.
I love it when we cuddle up in the bed,
The attraction is strong like two ends of a magnet,
Ready to connect.
Kissing you sends a jolt of excitement within me,
I love seeing thee,
The consumption of drugs could never satisfy me,
Because you're my addiction.

There's not a drug out there that can get me high,
But the look in your eyes,
The look of you being pleased as I stroke between your thighs.
I can only get drunk off of your love,
A kiss and a hug,
I look forward to you opening up like a rose bud.
Baby, sex with you gives me a rush,
There's no need to say word baby, just hush,
The only sounds necessary is my push, push,
You moaning louder as I grab on your tush.
Everything about you girl just blows my mind,
You stimulate me girl, all the time,
I love making love to you, because we're intertwined,
Always a different position, never a step behind,
Baby, you're my addiction.

Picture this baby, a spoon in a mug,
A clink, clink sound is being heard.
The spoon moves side to side and round and round,
Dip the spoon in and dip it back out,
Oh yes, that's how I get down.
I hope this analogy rings a bell,
A story to tell,
About how you and I are doing it well,
I'm about to bring back a word called swell,
Your moans turn to screams and screams to yells.
The only thing I roll, is you and I in the sheets,
Making your body weak,
Because of all your leaks,
You're unable to speak,
You're speech is impaired because I'm in to deep,
Why?
Because you're my addiction.

Yeah baby, you know it's you I like,
You make me smile, and drive me wild,
I want to rock your world,
Damn I love having you as my girl,
You're my addiction.

Set It Off

~Light the candles up, start the bath **water**,
Put on your lingerie, get the music **started**.
I'm coming into the room, with the cream and **fruit**,
I'll taste the fruit, and I'm tasting **you**.
That look in your eye, says let's get it **on**,
Take off your bra, and slide off your **thong**.

I want to set it off with **you**,
All I can think about is me sexing **you**.
Set it off with you my baby.
I want to set it off with **you**,
All I can think about is me sexing **you**.
Set it off with you my baby.

The bath overflows, because of all of them **suds**,
But we don't pay attention, because we're making **love**.
I'm getting into you, I mean I'm into **you**,
Forget everything else, focus on me and **you**.
There's no need to rush, we'll take it nice and **slow**,
It's music to my ears, when I hear you **moan**.

It's getting even later, but we keep on **going**,
Up top I'm kissing, but in the middle I'm **stroking**.
It's called body language, how we **communicate**,
Damn this feels so good, I found my **soul mate**.
You're on top of me, and then I'm on top of **you**,
Damn how I love, setting it off with **you**.

From your toes to,
Between your thighs and waistline,
Kissing until you tell me **stop**,
That's how I set it **off**.

I want to set it off with **you**,
All I can think about is me sexing **you**.
Set it off with you my baby.
I want to set it off with **you**,
All I can think about is me sexing **you**.
Set it off with you my baby.

Exotic

~There are several compliments one could use,
Ones that could lift your spirits when you're blue.
I must say that when it comes down to this girl,
She's unlike any other girl in this world.
If we were to awake in the morning and the sun were to die,
You could substitute her smile and it would be the light in our sky.
Her hair is as precious and valuable as silk,
Her personality could warm and comfort you like a quilt.
A sleek and exquisite figure she does possess,
Take a glance and your heart will beat out of your chest.
Her perfumes will have you sprung like a bee with flowers,
If you see her walk by, you'll be amazed for hours.
Her style, figure and beauty cannot be matched,
She should be a model, walking down a runway for people to watch.
She could put on this, and put on that,
She's exotic like I said, she looks good no matter what.
She's more than pretty, beautiful, sexy, cute or fine,
I call her all of these things and then some, and that's the exotic kind.

So Over You

~I've got to put those pictures of you away, now that we're **apart**,
Because whenever I look at them, I want to rip them all **apart**.
And I know that seems real harsh, because we had some real good **times**,
But it's how I feel since you broke that little heart of **mine**.
I always ask myself,
What in the world happened to **us**?
Was I to blame?
For our relationship to end in a **fuss**.
What could I have done?
To possibly change our relationship's **past**,
But it's over now, and I'm looking into the future and not the **past**.

You know I'm so over you girl,
I want nothing to do with **you**,
I'm so over the feelings that I used to have for **you**.
You know I'm so over you girl,
You are in the **past**,
So why do I still feel a little **sad**?

I try to erase those memories I had, those bad and those **good**,
The reason you gave for leaving, is still to me not **understood**.
Despite all of those things I did for you, you weren't **satisfied**,
I hope that you're feeling low, because my head is **high**.

You did me **wrong**,
But I am still **strong**.
I don't need none of your **love**,
Don't care to get your **hugs**,
I'm over you, I said I'm so over you.

You know I'm so over you girl,
I want nothing to do with **you**,
I'm so over the feelings that I used to have for **you**.
You know I'm so over you girl,
You are in the **past**,
So why do I still feel a little **sad**?

Just A Fling

~I loved her but she stabbed me in the **back**,
Stabbed me in the **back**,
I loved her but she stabbed me in the **back**,
Stabbed me in the **back**.

When we first met, I thought you were right for **me**,
But as it turned out, you didn't give a damn about **me**.
All the things I did for you, I thought it meant a lot to **you**,
But you just brushed it off, and kept playing me for a **fool**.
All the love I gave to you, you threw it all **away**,
And for that, it is you that I'll continue to **hate**.
When we held hands, I thought it meant **something**,
When you leaned over and kissed me, I thought it meant **something**,
When you said that you loved me, I thought it meant **something**,
But I realize, that to you, I meant **nothing**.

It was just a **fling**,
Girl you know I cared for you, had love for you, how could you do this to **me**.
It was just a **fling**,
We could've had something special girl, but instead you wanted to go and **deceive**.

I gave you so many gifts, I was your Santa **Claus**,
But what you gave me in the end, left me in a state of **pause**.
I used to brag about you to all of my **homeboys**,
And to your friends, you told them that I was your little **boy toy**.
They say what goes around comes back **around**,
And what goes up, must always come **down**.
Its messed up how you went and played with my **mind**,
I'm down right now, but when I rise, I'll be on the **grind**.

It was just a **fling**,
Girl you know I cared for you, had love for you, how could you do this to **me**.
It was just a **fling**,
We could've had something special girl, but instead you wanted to go and **deceive**.

18

Our Bond

~As I look into your eyes,
I cannot think to despise,
The sensation I get is of no surprise,
When we're intertwined between your thighs.
The love that I possess, is like no other,
I'm your umbrella, let me be your cover.
Your very presence brings excitement within me,
I love thee,
I'm devoted, and I will never leave,
Please believe,
My heart is what I will give thee,
I'm aimed to honor every one of your needs,
Emotionally,
Mentally,
I'm not all about pleasing physically,
My love for you is real, please believe.
You're one of a kind,
You always blow my mind,
I hope that we're together for all time,
I'm glad that you're mine,
You're the only jewel I need, go on and shine,
When our lips touch, I explode inside like a landmine.
I'm yours forever,
The love I have for you, nobody could measure,
If I'm a pirate, then you are my treasure.

As soon as I saw you,
I was immediately drawn to you,
From our first words, I knew that I wanted you.
Your voice is like music to my ears,
Don't shed any tears,
Have no fear,
For I will always be near.
I'm an artist, your body is a magnificent sculpture,
You being a model or winning pageants, I'm sure.
You're incredibly smart,
You're sweeter than a tart,
Every curve and crevice on your body is a work of art.
My love for you runs deep,
I would never think to cheat,
I don't need the tricks, I already have a treat,
You can't be beat,
Your status, other women cannot compete.
I love exploring that temple that is your body,
We both are nice people, but I love it when we're naughty.
Your mind, body and soul I want to explore,
It's you I adore,
If you're my addiction, I want more and more.

Taken

~There's something out there that I've noticed,
But it only seems to happen with the girl in my focus.
It always starts out with me meeting a girl,
And the girl just so happens to rock my world.
It's not just emotionally, mentally or maybe physically,
I'm a gentleman, for me, it's mainly about the personality.
We talk for awhile and things are moving right along,
I'm feeling this girl more and more, now my attraction is strong.
So far, things are going well, but wait, things are about to get better,
Our communication is consistent because we contact each other.
We communicate in many ways, online, phone calls and even texts,
It's things like this that put her ahead of the rest.
It doesn't matter, on the phone, online or in person, we talk for hours,
Not to mention that baby girl is as attractive as a beautiful flower.
Music, foods, movies, hobbies, morals, we have all of these in common,
That's why I desire her to be my woman.
Here's what I've noticed, a little problem always seems to occur,
There always seems to be a barrier that stops me from being with her.
The girl I like always seems to either not want a relationship or already has a boyfriend,
So then, all of my feelings, efforts and dreams all come to an end.
Is it convenience, karma, fate or just unlucky that this always happens to me?
The one girl I've desired, never, never, ever seems to be.
All of the conversations, moments and time spent together now won't help,
For she holds the cards and it's the friendship card that I was dealt.
I am striving for a relationship, but it's friendships I keep making,
I cannot reach my goal, if all of my desires are always taken.

The One That Got Away

~She was the one that got away,
She once was near, now she's too far away,
If I cared about her in that special way,
Then I shouldn't have let her go astray.
It was a long time ago, but it's fresh in my mind,
The one that's someone else's and should've been mine,
I can't believe I let a girl that was oh so fine,
Slip away and become another's bright sunshine.
The things she used to say, the things she used to do,
She was one of a kind, you'd miss her too.
We used to hang out, then we did a little more,
We once were friends, but I wished we were more.
The good times that we had, they were priceless,
There's no question, this girl, you bet I miss,
Oh how I wish,
I could just go back and get that one kiss,
Go back and give her sweet bliss.
Go back and whisper in her ear,
Go back and hold her and tell her to have no fear.
It's true what they say in all of those songs,
You don't know what you got 'til it's gone.
If I could turn back the hands of time,
She wouldn't be yours, instead, she'd be mine.

Fallin' For You

~I think that I'm fallin' for you,
Regardless of the fact that I just met you.
We've been talking for quite some time now,
Little did I know that once I saw you,
you would make me say wow.
Once you befriended me, I knew that I wanted to know more,
Still to this day, I don't know what could be in store.
There is so much about you that I already like,
From the way that you dress all the way to the look in your eyes.
When I first saw your picture, I was head over heels,
Darlin' you have no idea how you make me feel.
Every message received,
Had me filled with glee,
I still can't believe,
That a girl like thee,
So nice and sexy,
Is talking to me.
Nearly everything about you to me is ideal,
From the top of your head, to the bottom of your heels.
Your long dark hair that shines in the light,
Your gorgeous smile that glows so bright.
Your eyes that would make any man on Earth melt,
The nice, smooth, radiant skin that of the finest silk,
The cute dimples on your face and the ones on your lower back.

That runway walk of yours, yeah, I like that.
A midsection that would earn a perfect grade of an A,
The posterior, I hate to see you leave, but love to see you walk
away.
You have the legs of a world class model,
The way your body's shaped, it emulates the sleekest bottle.
How I would love to take a ride on all of your curves,
You'll have me saying, "thank you ma'am", I'll have you saying,
"thank you sir."
Your voice is as beautiful as an orchestrated symphony,
I don't know about y'all, but that's music to me.
I felt vibes being sent as if they were texts,
You definitely were the only girl around that had my interest.
I'm going to need CPR because of how you took my breath
away,
After meeting you, I could definitely chill with you all night and
all day.
You, my darlin', arise so many thoughts in this head of mine,
I only wish I knew if you share the same feelings as I.
Some may say it's too soon to feel like this,
But I can't help that you put me in a state of sensual bliss.
I have only but a few desires at this point in time,
One of which is to one day, make you mine.
What more can I say? What more can I do?
All I know is baby girl, I'm fallin' for you.

Break You Off

~You know how bad I want to make you soft,
Oh how I would love to break you off,
I'd be more than happy to pay the cost,
For the opportunity to break you off.
Doesn't matter day or night, or night or day,
Bluest skies or skies filled with cloudy gray.
From the warmest breeze to the coldest frost,
Oh how I really want to break you off.
I'd lay your body gently on the bed,
My magic will have your eyes rolled back in your head.
The feeling I'll give you will feel like a day in paradise,
Your body quivering as if it were cold as ice.
You're extremely turned on, you don't want me to stop,
I'll keep going until that moment when I break you off.
Seconds turn to minutes and minutes to hours,
Your whole body is glowing like a blooming spring flower.
I went from teasing, hugging, kissing and touching,
To squeezing, tugging, clinching and loving.
I'm aimed to please your body, from bottom to top,
Because that's what I'll do to break you off.
The time is not short and sweet, it's long and sweet,
Having you begging for more, asking me please and please,
I'm always in it to please,
I'm not in it to tease,
I'll do anything to give you a shake in your knees.
You know how bad I really want to get you soft,
Oh how I would really love to break you off.

The Other

~She calls me the other, what does that mean?
Does it mean that I am not what is to be?
I am not the primary,
Rather, I am the secondary.
Does she want me to be her number one?
To me, I already know that she's the one.
She has the body comparable to an hour glass,
The tension between us is thicker than molasses.
It is not bad tension, very good tension in fact,
Her partner, I'm sure, would not want to hear that.
Every time we see each other, a spark emerges,
Is it wrong of me to have these fantastical urges?
Doing this and that, and that and this,
I've thought of way more than just a sensual kiss.
When we chill together, we ride and we shine,
With her, it's impossible to not have a good time.
We go to this place and that place and this place again,
If I were to ever be with her, it would be an incredible win.
She has light, smooth skin that makes her gleam,
Her skin color reminds me of cookies and cream.
Is it wrong for me to think about her every day?
Is it wrong of me to think of her in every way?
I have so many things running through my mind,
One is the thought of one day, making you mine,
You're so divine,
You're one of a kind,
Other ladies you outshine,
When will it be my time?
I'll have to wait in line.

I'm no scientist, but I know that we have chemistry,
That partner that you have, I wish he were history.
I wonder if you believe we would be a perfect pair,
You could come to my lair,
I'll take you there,
Let me show you that I care,
You girl, I don't want to share.
Those other guys, they're like peons to me,
They don't want you as bad as me,
They won't care for you like me,
They won't love you like me,
They can't hug you like me,
Or touch you like me,
Kiss you like me,
Or even sex you like me.
You do a lot for me just by me seeing your face,
If I'm a deck of cards, I want you to be my ace.
The things that he's put you through,
I would never do to you,
I'm the king and I want my queen to be you.
I hope you feel close to me,
Because I feel close to thee,
I'm not saying you should leave him, but you need to like,
roll with me.
I love it when we get a chance to roll out and mingle,
Damn, how I wish that you were single.
Some say I shouldn't think about you in these ways,
But I can't help daydreaming of you all through the day.

Mi Chia

~It was the break of dawn,
When I finally saw,
The woman that makes me stand in awe,
She knows my name, but it's another she wanted to call,
So this new name of mine had just been spawned,
This made me stand all proud and tall.
Her "chio" is what she wanted my title to be,
And since I did not disagree,
I gladly agreed,
In fact, I was filled with glee,
That this wonderful lady,
Wanted me to fit this title so willfully.
Why so excited you may ask? One might understand,
If you were to just take a glance,
At this woman at hand.
She has eyes you melt into,
Skin ever so smooth,
And she doesn't mind getting down into a groove,
She has golden hair to run your fingers through,
Her face is real cute too,
She always smells as good as the freshest fruit,
The body of a Greek statue,
Juicy lips in fact too,
Quite frankly to sum it up, this girl is beautiful.

She's tropical, the very definition of exotic,
It can be so erotic,
The way she can move her body is hypnotic.
When she speaks to me, it sounds like the music of instruments,
If she opens her cabinet,
I'll be her chocolate and her my cinnamon,
Whether we're in a house, a condo or an apartment,
Forget those other men,
She should choose me, because I'm the only real specimen.
When it comes to her, she's always in my dreams,
She's the M.V.P.,
Because every man wants her on their team,
I want her to be my queen,
At least that's how I would treat thee,
Forget making her yell, with me I'll make her scream.
She gave me a name, and I have one for her right back,
Especially since she called me her "chio", and I kind of like that,
I now name her "mi chia", because she's got it like that,
Us being together is what's left on tap.
Quiero ser contigo siempre, mi chia,
Porque usted es tan bella.

25

To Be Honest

~To be honest…I am very glad that we **met**,
To be honest…since then, you've taken my **breath**.
To be honest…I feel so comfortable around **you**,
To be honest…no one makes me feel the way you **do**.
To be honest…you are very **considerate**,
To be honest…it is you that is my **favorite**.
To be honest…I have feelings for **you**,
To be honest…I desire no one else but **you**,
To be honest…I love so many things about **you**,
To be honest…I hope and pray you feel the same way I **do**.
To be honest…I think you are top of the **book**,
To be honest…I'm mesmerized by your exotic **look**.
To be honest…I think so highly of **thee**,
To be honest…the one who should be with you is **me**,
To be honest…you fill me with so much **glee**,
To be honest…I will remember you for all **eternity**,
To be honest…you have given me so many good **memories**,
To be honest…my feelings for you grow like that of **weeds**.
To be honest…my feelings for you have reached all new **heights**,
To be honest…all I need is you to be my **sunlight**,
To be honest…I think that you are such a pretty **sight**,
To be honest…the way I feel about you is beyond the word **like**.
To be honest…you have shown me so many **things**,
To be honest…you shine brighter than any diamond **ring**.
To be honest…every time I am with you I am **happy**,
To be honest…I would scream how I feel until my voice was **raspy**.
To be honest…so many things about you I enjoy so **much**,
To be honest…it ranges from the sound of your voice to your very **touch**.
To be honest…I hope you accept the fact that I feel this **way**,
To be honest…I want you to know I mean everything that I **say**.
To be honest…I do not have a lot of **time**,
To be honest…I will spend every last second trying to make you **mine**.

Love It

~There's so much that I love about **you**,
I cannot express it all in just one word or **two**.
There are several places where I could **begin**,
Let me first admire your smooth, silky **skin**.
A baby's bottom could not even **compare**,
To your beautiful skin that I kiss and touch with **care**.
From the skin on the bottom of your feet to your forehead up **top**,
Every inch of your body is covered with skin that is so **soft**.
The finest orchestra in the world could not come close to **play**,
Music so relaxing as your voice when you speak the words you **say**.
I get intrigued by your whispers in my ear and its **content**,
My hair stands on its end at the very hint of your sexy **accent**.
Your golden hair I admire for its look and because it is **versatile**,
Your hair looks incredibly beautiful and elegant no matter the **style**.
Nothing can give me a warmer feeling inside me than to see your **smile**,
The thought of me making you smile just drives me **wild**.
Your very touch soothes my whole body, both inside and **out**,
My body yearns for your touch, there is no **doubt**.
When God has a good day, he has one **indeed**,
He had his best day when he decided to create **thee**.
That figure you possess, it is like no **other**,
A body such as yours should never be **covered**,
At the very chance to become yours, my love for you I would **smother**,
The feelings I have for you are so deep, it cannot go any **further**.
There are meanings behind words and words are defined by **meanings**,
I have said and thought many things, but just remember one **thing**.
No matter who you're with or where you are, I won't be **afar**,
I will always remember you because I love who you **are**.
All these things I have said about you, I love them, I really **do**,
But what I really want to say is that darlin', I love **you**.

Irreplaceable

I love her swagger and she loves mine too,
That's why no other woman could ever fill your shoes,
Girl it's true,
Nobody but you,
Could ever make me feel the way you do,
You know who I'd choose,
Between someone else and you,
I'd scream over and over, "Yes I pick you",
Me, replacing you?
That I could never do,
Irreplaceable is how I would define you,
When I say this, this is true,
A perfect duo me and you,
If all the others can't see it, then they need to get a clue,
To find someone like you,
There are only a few,
Matter of fact, there's no one else as special as you,
I'd say this to you,
No one else but you,
I'd tell you how I really feel about you,
What have I got to lose,
No need to hide the truth,
For it is I that is the one that truly loves you,
So if you're ever sad and blue,
No that this little thing is true,
I could never, never, ever replace you.

Rescue

-I'm thinking about your salvation,
If I succeed, I'll need a standing ovation.
I'm a normal man, not a super hero,
Nevertheless, this is what I want you to know,
See I think that you're incredibly special,
And that your guy is the one you should let go.
He doesn't see you in the light that I do,
He doesn't appreciate you like I do,
He doesn't look at you the way that I do,
Ain't no way he loves you more than I do,
You're being held captive by this lame dude,
Therefore it is I that will come to your rescue.
I'm willing to do anything to sweep you off your feet,
The way you make me feel gives me a really fast heartbeat,
He should stay out of the kitchen, because he can't stand the heat,
Come get with a winner and you could never be beat.
I'll climb any mountain, swim across any sea,
Quite frankly, I'll do anything just to be with thee.
In this story he's the villain and I'm the good guy,
You're a priceless commodity that money could never buy.
I'll rob from the rich and give to the poor,
I'll always fight for your love, no matter the score.
Nor a bird, nor a plane, no none of the above,
I've come to rescue you and give you all of my love.
I'm your knight in shining armor, baby take me as I am,
Because I want you to be my girl and I want to be your man.

Don't Go

-One of the best things that's ever happened to me,
Was the very moment that I laid eyes on thee.
We met each other, an introduction was made,
You intrigued me, therefore my full attention I gave.
We began to talk and we began to mingle,
By this time, you don't know how bad I want you to be single.
First we started talking, then we started texting,
The notion of being your man would be the ultimate blessing.
We would take turns, I take you out, you take me out,
It doesn't matter where we go, as long as we're out and about.
Quite some time has passed and we've grown even closer,
By now the only thing on my mind is my desire to hold her.
We would see each other several times throughout the week,
To not see or talk to her would make my body weak.
Make me weak in the knees,
Make it so I can't even breathe,
She makes me feel as good as a cool summer breeze,
She's my voice when I speak,
My eyes when I blink,
She's the blood running through my veins when my heart beats.
Without her is like a car without its wheels,
From your man, it is you that I would like to steal.
I don't want you to leave, girl I want you to stay,
That's the way I would want it, if I had it my way.
I will cherish all of our memories from beginning to end,
If you do leave, I'll always dream of seeing you once again.
Whether you stay or you leave, I want you to know,
In my heart you will stay with me, but I don't want you to go.

Intimacy

~It gets more amazing every single **time**,
I just love how we both **unwind**.
I love how I get to hold you close to **me**,
I could look into your eyes for an **eternity**,
How I yearn for you to touch **me**,
When you do, a warm feeling takes over **me**,
It doesn't matter where we might **be**,
Whether on the sofa or underneath the **sheets**,
I'll find any way I can to please **thee**,
You can damn well bet that you can please **me**.
I pull you close to me and kiss **you**,
I have discovery hands, they want to explore **you**,
Just looking at you can put me in the **mood**,
When we kiss, I love it when I taste **you**,
I just can't help myself whenever I touch **you**,
Every curve and crevice of your body is so **smooth**.
I can't wait to lay your body **down**,
What happens is your light skin underneath my **brown**.
I undo each button and zipper real **slow**,
You're liking what I'm doing so you never say **no**.

I take your clothes off and throw them across the **room**,
If you don't know by now, I'm really into **you**.
I waste no time to get **inside**,
You squeeze my waist real tight with your **thighs**.
I'm good at moving in all sorts of **motions**,
Making your body wet just like an **ocean**.
While we're engaged we have **conversations**,
Everything we're doing right now is **titillating**.
We put our tongues on each other like **lollipops**,
The way you make me feel baby don't you ever **stop**.
Spread eagle for me and I'll make you **fly**,
It doesn't matter, I can be in or **outside**.
I would taste you every day that I **could**,
Because baby girl, you're finger-lickin' **good**.
By now you know that I have talented **hands**,
These things will happen as long as I'm your **man**.
I'm addicted to only one thing and that's your **love**,
Everything from making love to a simple **hug**.
All day and night I could make love to **thee**,
Together we construct the best **intimacy**.

31

What Love Is

~Gazing into each others' eyes,
Doing what I can to make you mine,
Is this what love is?
Seeing you every chance that I get,
Trying to become the one you'll never forget,
Is this what love is?
Being that shoulder that you can lean on,
Being the main one that you can count on,
Apologizing for the times that I am wrong,
Missing you deeply whenever you are gone,
Is this what love is?
Anticipating your every text or call,
Wanting not just a piece of you, but all,
Being there to help you rise when you fall,
Is this what love is?
Comforting you when you are sick or down,
Knowing that if you need me, I will be around,
Being the real man you need and not a clown,
Helping turn all your frowns upside down,
Is this what love is?

Being there to accompany you when you take a bath,
Whenever you are stressed, I will massage your back,
Is this what love is?
Listening to you whenever you speak,
Helping to take a load off of your feet,
Not being selfish, thinking of you not me,
Is this what love is?
Me desiring to show you love, even in public,
Me kissing and touching you softly, easy does it,
Is this what love is?
Me always wanting to give you the proper love and affection,
Helping to guide you in the right direction,
Giving you, my angel, the necessary protection,
Is this what love is?
My aim to please you to the fullest, I will keep it going,
The sight of waking up next to you in the morning.
All of these things I have mentioned I truly adore,
It is not just these things, there are many more.
To answer the question of is this what love is?
Yes, I am with you and I have found what true love is.

Lost & Found

-You have caught my eye,
I want you to be mine,
I once was lost, but now I'm found.
I love the time we spend,
I never want it to end,
I once was lost, but now I'm found.
All of the moments we've shared,
I will cherish with care,
I once was lost, but now I'm found.
We were together one minute,
Then lost you the next instant,
I once was found, but now I'm lost.
Just to hear your voice,
Makes me rejoice,
I once was lost, but now I'm found.
I love interacting with you my dear,
Why must they interfere?
I once was found, but now I'm lost.
I've fallen so deep in love,
You're my angel from above,
I once was lost, but now I'm found.
I'm the one that wants you,
But he's the one who has you,
I once was found, but now I'm lost.
He has given you nothing,
I'll give you my everything,
I am neither lost nor found.
You are the love of my life,
I yearn for you to be my wife,
I once was lost, but now I'm found.
It is hard for me,
It is hard for thee,
Without you I'm lost, but with you I'm found.

33

My Pain

~I feel it when you are away,
I feel this in every way,
I feel this every day,
Will my pain ever go away?
At night I cannot sleep,
I miss hearing you speak,
Without you I am weak,
Will my pain ever go away?
I love you the way you are,
I miss you when we are apart,
I want you near and never far,
Will my pain ever go away?
I miss feeling your touch,
I miss us doing such and such,
Everything about you I miss so much,
Will my pain ever go away?
I think about you every day and night,
Being with you, it just feels so right,
How I miss holding you so tight,
Will my pain ever go away?
I am grateful that you were born,
Whenever I am with you I am never bored,
Every second without you hurts me more and more,
Will my pain ever go away?
Not hearing your voice is like having deaf ears,
Rain pouring from the sky describes my tears,
Losing you forever is what I fear,
Will my pain ever go away?
Having my loving heart be severed,
Loving another as I do you, never,
Having the love of my life gone forever,
Will my pain ever go away?
No one makes me feel the way you do,
It is I that wants to be with you,
It is impossible for another to love you the way I do,
How I hope and pray that my pain goes away.

How I Feel

~I've never felt like this before,
It's you that I truly adore,
You are everything I need and more,
This is how I feel.
You are not beautiful, but far beyond,
Our love is more magical than a wand,
You and I share a special bond,
This is how I feel.
I love the time we spend,
I never want our relationship to end,
It is you that is my perfect ten,
This is how I feel.
Everything about you just drives me wild,
You can light up the world with your gorgeous smile,
I love your classy and sexy style,
This is how I feel.
I want to be with no one else,
I do not need anyone else,
I just want you all to myself,
This is how I feel.
I desperately want you in my life,
It is you that I want to make my wife,
You truly are the love of my life,
This is how I feel.

Without You

~A yard with no fence,
A flower with no scent,
This is my life without you.
The sky without clouds,
Having no ups, but downs,
This is my life without you.
Adam without Eve,
A tree with no leaves,
This is my life without you.
Things being wrong and not right,
Eyes without sight,
A sun that's not bright,
This is my life without you.
A car without wheels,
My world at a stand still,
This is my life without you.
An army without guns,
The morning without the sun,
This is my life without you.
A king without his crown,
Me always feeling down,
This is my life without you.
I don't know what I would do,
If I had to live my life without you.

Makin' Love

~I'm getting extreme butterflies,
Just by gazing in your eyes,
Whenever I'm with you, I'm on cloud nine.
The look in your eye is saying take me,
The look in my eye is telling you that you have me,
Just looking at you makes me desire thee.
I grab a hold of your body and pull you close,
If I need medicine, your body's my dose,
Every time I get to hold you, I feel the need to boast.
I close my eyes as I kiss on your lips,
I pull you closer as I grab on your hips,
Oh how I love exploring your body with my fingertips.
We continue kissing each other as I lay you down,
We take off our shoes and let them hit the ground,
I keep kissing your lips, then neck and work my way down.
I take off your shirt and unbuckle your belt,
How I'm about to make you feel, you have never felt,
With just one touch, you can make me melt.
I kiss on your neck, then move to your chest,
I take off your bra and lay it to rest,
How I love tasting your nipples and caressing your breasts.
You unbuckle my belt and pull my shirt off,
You grab me by my arms and pull me on top,
I'm beginning to sweat and not because it is hot.
I kiss on your stomach as I slide off your pants,
You're caressing my body with your smooth and soft hands,
Damn how I love that you chose me as your man.
Off come my jeans and off come your panties,
No one else in sight, so we have our privacy,
Makin' love to you is so exciting.

How do you like it, you can bet that I know,
I enter it in fast instead of sliding it in slow,
It's music to my ears to hear you moan.
You know that I love it when we do what we do,
It feels so good, so right, when I'm inside you,
We belong together, we both know that it's true.
You're feeling me go up and down and in and out,
Your moans turn to screams and they become loud,
Pleasing my woman, that's what I'm all about.
I'll keep going and going in all types of positions,
Whenever you make a sound, I'll be sure to listen,
You love it when I sweat and my body glistens.
You're the only one that can get me solid as a rock,
You turn me over and now you're on top,
Baby you feel so good, I don't want you to stop.
The way you ride me is like you were in a rodeo,
You're my Juliet, let me be your Romeo,
I want to make love to you every time I get a hold of you.
You're so tight, so warm, so wet, I love it,
You feel so good to me that I want more of it,
If I could not have you, then I would have a fit.
I love tasting you, because you taste so good,
I would taste you every chance that I got if I could,
You and I together forever, it's understood.
We're still going at it, you're now on your back,
I'm not done loving you yet, I need no slack,
I'll go harder and deeper until you climax.
Once we do, we hold each other and then relax.
Damn how I love makin' love to you,
This is only one of the many reasons why I love you.

Missing You

~You are the air I need in which to breathe,
You are my eyes in which I need to see.
You are my one and only love that is true,
This is why I am missing you.
You are the sun that is in my sky,
Seeing you brings a twinkle to my eye.
I am my happiest when I am with you,
This is why I am missing you.
Without you my world is at a stand still,
No one makes me feel the way you make me feel.
I am my most comfortable when I am around you,
This is why I am missing you.
I want to be with you at all costs,
Without you I am lost.
There is not a moment that I do not think of you,
This is why I am missing you.
It is you that I adore,
Every moment I spend with you makes me yearn for you more and more.
For all eternity I want to be with you,
Until we reunite, I will continue to miss you.

Being Away From You

~I cannot stand being away from you,
Because now I don't know what to do.
I hate you being so far away,
How bad I want you to come back and stay,
I will always be with you, I will never stray,
I will be here waiting for you every night and day.
It is only you that is on my mind,
It is only you that I desire to be mine.
It is like a knife going through my back,
You do not know how badly I want you to come back.
You could never imagine how much I am missing you,
I just want to be with you and make your dreams come true.
You are all that I want and all that I need,
I am blind to everyone else, it is only you that I see.
With you I am something,
Without you I am nothing.
With you my darlin', you make me feel nourished,
The very thought of not being with you makes me feel deserted.
You are everything I need and more,
I love having you to adore.
I will do anything in this world to get you,
I will do whatever it takes to keep you.
It is you that is my future, never mind the past,
What it is that we have, I know it will last.
No one in this world makes me feel the way you do,
That is why I hate being away from you.

Why Me?

~Why me?
Why can I not seem to get a **break?**
Why is so much negativity surrounding me?
Why do things always seem to happen to me?
Why do I continue to experience so much pain and **ache?**
Why is it that I continue to do all of the right things,
Only to receive bad things in **return?**
It is hard to keep my spirits up,
When I continue to get **burned.**
Why do I even **try?**
Why continue to be genuine?
What is even the point?
It can be so hard to take, that sometimes I want to **cry.**
With every single negative,
My confidence takes a **hit.**
Everyone has their boiling point,
Before they say, "That's **it**".
I've dealt with the strife, I've dealt with the **pain.**
I've experienced heartbreak and I've dealt with loss.
It doesn't seem to matter how much effort I put in,
I continue to struggle, struggle in **vain.**
They say good things come to those who wait.
When will it finally be my turn to have good things come my **way?**
They say patience is a virtue and I've waited all of my life.
Is there light at the end of the tunnel? I'll see, one **day.**

I Miss...

~Words cannot express how much I miss her
I miss the way she used to look at me...
I miss her vibrant smile...
I miss making her laugh...
I miss her fresh aroma whenever she was close to me...
I miss the way she would squeeze me tight when we hugged...
I miss feeling her warm, soft, juicy lips
against mine when we kissed...
I miss running my fingers through her hair...
I miss the fun that we used to have...
I miss taking her out to dinner...
I miss us seeing movies together...
I miss coming by to visit her...
I miss her coming by to visit me...
I miss seeing her come around the corner...
I miss the way she would look at me when we were lying in bed...
I miss her touching my face while looking at me...
I miss feeling her hands caress my body...
I miss running my fingers across every curve
and crevice of her body...
I miss her nibbling on my ear...
I miss her whispering in my ear...
I miss me holding her from behind...

I miss hearing her call my name...
I miss the things that we used to do...
I miss the conversations that we used to have...
I miss us reminiscing about old times...
I miss hearing her calming voice...
I miss the fact that she wanted to always be around me...
I miss her glowing every time that she saw me...
I miss waking up in the morning next to her...
I miss being intimate with her...
I miss my best friend...
I miss my soul mate...
I miss my heart...
I miss the letters she would write to me...
I miss us going out together...
I miss being able to hold her hand...
I miss us riding in the car together...
I miss us being together...
I miss seeing her every day...
I miss the love of my life...
I miss us...
But what I truly miss the most...
Is YOU!

41

A Blessing

~She was sent from above, down here to me,
Never would I have imagined meeting someone as she,
I have no need to search, for I have already found my destiny,
I know deep down inside that she was meant for me,
I'm in love with thee,
It's plain to see,
Even the blind can see,
It's no mystery,
It is her that completes me,
It is her that makes me happy,
It is her that I wish to marry,
My baby I want her to carry,
To me there's only you, there's no need to worry,
There are no others, they don't exist to me,
To me, you are lovely,
To me you are lively,
Being with me, I thank you kindly,
You are the beholder of my heart, my one true entity,
It is you that I choose to be my queen,
I thank the Lord above for blessing me,
With the woman that I love and in return, loves me.

Love Angel

~To my baby from across the **way**,
I want you to know that I would never **stray**,
Even if we might be miles **away**,
It is your name that I will always **say**,
It doesn't matter if there's sunshine or **rain**,
I will be there to warm you like a mug of **café**.
I knew from the start that you were sent from **above**,
That, among other things, made me fall in **love**.
It's more than just intimacy, we've got a **connection**,
Please be my angel and I'll be your **protection**.
I'll do more than soothe your body, I'll put your mind and soul at **rest**,
I'm your breath of fresh air, I am better than the **rest**,
I'm willing to work hard for you baby, so put me to your **test**,
You're not rolling with second or third, you're rolling with the **best**,
I have so much that I want to offer, more than anyone could ever **harvest**,
I'm here to relieve you of your pain, not administer any **stress**.
Others may be blind to this fact, but I can see your **halo**,
My feelings for you I have to reveal, they cannot just lay **low**.
You're as angelic as they come, it's just that **simple**,
You're not ordinary or plain, you're as fine as **crystal**.
From above I saw you coming straight from heaven's **door**,
Ever since that day, I've wanted you more and **more**.
The only feeling I have for you within me is **love**,
I thank the Lord that he sent you to me from **above**.

Letting Go(One & Only Special Love)

~Our one and only special love,
I'm feeling like you're letting go,
Our one and only special love,
I'm feeling like you're letting go.
It's been so very long since I've seen your **face**,
Now I'm standing before you, face to **face**.
I reach out to hug you, kiss you and **hold you**,
But something is telling me this isn't the same **old you**.
Seeing you in the flesh just makes me **glow**,
Your glow seems faint, why? I don't **know**.
Our one and only special love,
I'm feeling like you're letting go,
Our one and only special love,
I'm feeling like you're letting go.
All of this time we've been apart, it is I that has **missed you**,
I'm happy to say that I held, hugged and **kissed you**.
You've been going through some things,
I'm here to bring you **up**,
You lacking positive notions, I'm here to fill your **cup**.
Whatever you need, I was there to give you a **boost**,
Because you and your love, I never want to **lose**.
Our one and only special love,
I'm feeling like you're letting go,
Our one and only special love,
I'm feeling like you're letting go.
I came to bring you all of my love, happiness and **passion**,
Then you pull me aside and tell me
that you just don't **have it**.
You tell me that I'm special, tell me that I'm **perfect**,

Then you try to tell me that you don't want to **hurt me**.
I start to see your **tears**,
Now I'm in **fear**,
Concerned about what it is I'm going to **hear**.
Our one and only special love,
I'm feeling like you're letting go,
Our one and only special love,
I'm feeling like you're letting go.
You told me that you need me, told me that you **love me**,
Then turn around and say that you do not **deserve me**.
You said that all of this time, you've been bringing me **down**,
You weren't bringing me down before, but you have **now**.
You said that you've lost some of the passion and fire **within**,
You don't want me as your man, but certainly your **friend**.
Our one and only special love,
I'm feeling like you're letting go,
Our one and only special love,
I'm feeling like you're letting go.
After hearing your words, tears begin to fall down my **cheek**,
Then my body, even my heart starts to grow **weak**.
After all that we have been through,
all that we went **through**,
All the love that you gave me, my all that I gave **you**.
I believe in fighting for that special **one**,
Fighting for the one you **love**,
Not giving up and letting go of a true **love**.
Our one and only special love, I feel like you let it go,
Our one and only special love, I feel like you let it go.

LaVergne, TN USA
23 January 2011
213656LV00002B